Made in the USA
Columbia, SC
25 May 2025

CONTACT

EMAIL
INFO@DESTINYINSPIRE.COM

WEB
WWW.DESTINYINSPIRE.COM

DESTINY INSPIRE

AUTHOR| SPEAKER |COACH
The Empowerment Juggernaut

@DESTINY_INSPIRE   @DESTINYINSPIRE   @DESTINYINSPIRE1

AVAILABLE FOR:
- CONFERENCES
- KEYNOTES
- WORKSHOPS
- SEMINARS
- CHURCHES
- SCHOOLS
- YOUTH GROUPS

SPECIALIZING IN:
- ONE-ON-ONE COACHING
- GROUP COACHING
- PERSONAL DEVELOPMENT
- GOAL SETTING
- STRATEGY AND EXECUTION
- OVERCOMING OBSTACLES

Acknowledgements

It is with so much joy that I am able to fulfill my life's purpose with impacting women around the globe. I am so full seeing lives transformed with the power of my personal, practical, and empowering principles. I am extremely grateful to God for gracing me with the many gifts he has given to me. I owe him everything! Everything I do is that my life would bring him joy and my light will win him souls.

I also want to take a moment to acknowledge a few more individuals who have played an impactful and intricate role in my life.

To my loving parents David and Mary Kingcannon who began this legacy long before I ever came to be. Thank you for your unwavering love and acceptance of this journey I am on. It is your prayers and support that have kept me grounded.

To every queen that makes up The Queen Counsel, I honor you. For your dedication and support you are appreciated. For allowing me to purely pour into you everything that the father imparts into me. To see the growth and development in each of you does my heart good and makes this all worth it.

To each of my mentors who lovingly refine me by challenging me and chiseling me. It is with your help and support that I am able to uncover the precious masterpiece that lies underneath. For every text, call, and message that each of you have afforded me to learn and grow. For seeing greater in me at times than I even saw in myself. Thank you for molding me to never settle for mediocrity!

Table of Contents

Dedication: 1

Introduction 3

Chapter1: Defining The Decision 5

Chapter 2: The Self-Love Solution 10

Chapter 3: Key 1: Silence Negative Self Talk 15

Chapter 4: Key 2: Affirm & Confirm 22

Chapter 5: Key 3: Navigate Something New 28

Chapter 6: 4 Find A Positive Posse................................32

Chapter 7: Key 5: Honor Your Health 37

Chapter 8: Key 6: Ignore Negativity 41

Chapter 9: Key 7: Expect The Best.................................44

Dedication:

I would like to dedicate this book to the younger version of me. To the Destiny who never imagined this is the woman she would be. To the Destiny who once couldn't even dream of her own destiny.

To the Destiny who struggled with her own self-worth. May you now know that God has had his hand on you since birth.

I would also like to dedicate this book to the person reading this who has the audacity to believe that whatever they have the capacity to believe, they will undoubtedly be able to achieve.

May these 7 keys unlock the very self-confidence that you need.

Confidence is not walking in a room thinking, I hope they like me. Confidence is walking in room knowing, I will be ok even if they don't."~ Destiny Inspire

INTRODUCTION

Often times we struggle with the concept of accomplishments. Deep down inside I firmly believe that we know there is a greater purpose in our lives that we should be living. However, what we display and the life we choose to live is indicative of how we see ourselves. This as a result governs not only what we accomplish, but how we interact and even engage with others. We place others on superficial pedestals, as if we don't possess the same power to pursue the purpose in our own lives.

While I make no claims to be the most self-confident woman in the world, I do firmly believe that my life experiences and work in my field of work have all contributed to being able to provide insight that will assist you. In my time with coaching women into discovering their purpose and assisting them as they create plans of action to accomplish their goals, there are a few things that I have deduced.

1. You don't lack the skills and abilities to accomplish things in your life. You lack unlocking what's needed in order to execute those things.
2. One of the biggest issues is not understanding the pivotal importance of producing purpose through gaining self-confidence.
3. The lack of self-confidence prohibits you from considering the possibilities that are surrounding your life and the calling you are designed to accomplish with your life.

This book was written as a tool to help you get out of your own way! This resource is designed to provide you with a safe space to self-reflect. It will present you with practical principles that will help produce or enhance the self-confidence needed to pursue so much more. It will help you with removing the limits off your heart and mind and tapping into the unlimited resources already on the inside of you and available to you.

If you will, open up your heart and allow this book to help you see yourself in a way you otherwise would never have considered before. Once you have done so, you will then be commissioned to return the favor, and share this book with someone who needs to tap into the confidence needed to conquer their calling. I will add that it is important to answer the reflection. These questions will help you facilitate the process of growth and change in your life. Within you lies deep answers. You only need to dig deeper to pull them out. So, make sure you are intentional about taking the time to coach yourself through these questions. I am here with you on this limitless journey.

CHAPTER 1

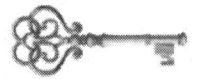

DEFINING THE DECISION

Self-Confidence (N) The Ability to Trust Your Powers, Abilities, Judgement, And Yourself.

In a world where social media allows us to present ourselves in a post that doesn't really portray the real person, it becomes easy to pretend we possess a level of self-confidence that we really and truly do not have. The worst part about it is that we have fallen into a deep pit and swallowed the potion that has convinced us we should simply "Just fake it until we make it." The problem with this is we never really make it. At least unless we are completely intentional about taking the necessary action steps in order to make it.

But what if, just what if, you actually knew how to develop the faculty of your personality to truly be the confident person you are supposed to be?

Let's be honest, there is so much more we would do, say, or accomplish, if we had the self-confidence to do so.

We would start the business, apply for that position, stand up for ourselves, shoot that relational shot, and just dominate in our life! Too often we look at others and say, "What if?"

Instead of looking within and saying, "I can!" We pretend and look at others as if they are super-human and possess mutant abilities that are not possible for us. Now, of course, you have those phenomenal people and athletes such as Usain Bolt, the fastest man in the world, or others who have amazing talents. But for the most part, we all have a specific unique thing about us that no one else can duplicate. So whether or not we possess the attributes or qualities of someone else, we do possess the infinite mental capacity to think deeper, believe better, and live louder. We only need to convince ourselves that there is greatness on the inside of us. This won't happen by accident. This will only happen with intentionality an and understanding of who we are and what we are capable of.

My shero the late Dr. Maya Angelou, oftentimes in her talks spoke of a quote by a once enslaved turned Roman African playwright, known as "Terrance."

"If a human being dreams a great dream, dares to

love somebody; if a human being dares to be Martin King, or Mahatma Gandhi, or Mother Theresa, or Malcolm X; if a human being dares to be bigger than the condition into which she or he was born-it means so can you. And so you can try to stretch, stretch, stretch yourself so you can internalize, 'Homo sum, humani nil a me alienum puto. I am a human being, nothing human can be alien to me.' That's one thing I'm learning. Maya Angelou

What is capable of being done for someone else is a testament that it can be done in anyone. We need only to believe that because within us dwells the duality of both natural and super! For starters, I am a woman of faith, and I firmly believe that we are triune beings, that we are a spirit, we have a soul, and we live within a body. We just tend to get stuck on being a body that's full of soulish emotions. We never acknowledge the spirit side of us that supersedes anything carnal. The side of us that when we tap into something greater than ourselves, or as a person of faith, someone who is the all-powerful God, you realize that there is nothing that cannot be achieved or accomplished. We just need not to be afraid or comfortable where we are.

We limit our own growth and our abilities when we choose to only play it safe. Sometimes playing it safe is also playing it small. You have so much potential inside of you that's just waiting to be tapped into and executed.

You are royalty and you were made to conquer. It's important to stop letting a lack of self-confidence hold you back. It's time for you to trust yourself. Believe in yourself. You've got this! You were made in the image of the divine. There were no mistakes made there. Nothing about your life is a mistake. You now need to open your eyes and see yourself the way the creator saw His creation when He said, "It is very good."

What I'm about to present to you caters to a curriculum that will help curate good character while cultivating your confidence at the same time. It's time you become productive and prosperous in all areas of life to include both personal and professional.

"I AM ME! That is the greatest person I could ever be."
Destiny Inspire

Chapter 2

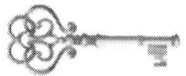

THE SELF-LOVE SOLUTION

Before we can talk about having self-confidence, we have to discuss reasons why we struggle to gain self-confidence.

Can I submit to you that one of the reasons I have discovered that we lack self-confidence, is due to the fact we have not grasped the concept of self- love? I also should add, you cannot love yourself, unless you know yourself or your identity. That is going to have to be the foundation upon which everything else will build upon. (Self-discovery and identity which I covered in my last book "Discovering Destiny: A 31-Day Guide to Finding Yourself and Fulfilling Your Purpose." That would also be an additional resource that you are more than welcomed to visit to help bring continuity to self-confidence.)

Now I know you got this book with the intent you would find out all things confidence. But we have to be completely honest with ourselves, and first address the foundational problem that is posed before ever actualizing self-confidence.

True self-confidence can only be rooted in love of self. If that is complicated to conceptualize then just reverse the word around to read as the love of self! Now I am not just referring to the millennial redefinition of self-love flossed on Facebook by false fingernails and by pictures of bubble baths. I am talking about the love that you can only give to yourself when you appreciate, honor, respect, and believe in yourself. The love that self-affirms and validates, that will therefore, reflect in the self-care that you see. When self-love becomes an actual practice and not just a pleasant principle, it then develops into confidence.

Ask me how I know…

I know this because I had to address the lack thereof in my own life. I have not begun my life as the confident "Empowerment Juggernaut," that I am now known as. I was once like many reading this book, battling the insecurities that came to attach and attack any ounce of hope for a brighter future that I had. I once felt unnecessary. I felt that my life really did not have anything greater. So, I did not really have the confidence to accomplish things. I would look at other people and marvel at the things they could do, create, and become. Deep on the inside, I wanted to become more, do more, be more... But instead, I wore the concept of not being enough. Maybe that mindset came from moments in my life that made me feel like I could not measure up to most.

I once heard Willie Moore Jr use the expression, "We meander in the maze of mediocrity." I've learned as it pertained to my own life, that it could not be truer. I had to tell myself that "it's mediocre to allow your mind to wonder whether or not you are good enough. It's mediocre to make idols out of icons, to search for validation, affirmation, and confirmation from people who were also just as self-conscious." What I must remind you, is that other people loving you is a bonus, but learning to truly love yourself, that is the real blessing. Not only that, but I had to affirm myself that *"You possess everything you need to become the woman of your own dreams. You are more than what you've been through. It's Time for you to see the real you!"*

Just like me, you may need to come to these realizations in order to begin your journey of manifestation into unlocking the keys to self-confidence. You may be reading this right now and asking yourself, "Am I meandering in mediocrity, or am I measuring up to who I am meant to be?" When we truly love ourselves, we will be able to believe in ourselves. To love yourself is to believe in yourself. It is with boldness that we use that belief in order to continue to be who we were created to be.

I want to dismantle the notion that having self-love is selfish. The greatest book ever given to mankind reads to "Love others as you love yourself." (Mark 12:31). Now that sounds pretty simple, but what we seem to miss is that, in order to love others the best way we can, we have to first identify how much do we really love ourselves. We also have to identify that many times our actions towards others are also indicative of our actions and love for ourselves. How is it possible to truly love someone else with a love that you yourself do not possess nor demonstrate for yourself? It is therefore vital to evaluate our devotion in loving ourselves in a way that will reflect in the way we love others. When we effectively love ourselves, we will have confidence within, which is not to be confused with conceit.

Self-love and self-confidence do not work independently of each other. They collaborate to help create the kind of person you have been commissioned to be from the very beginning of creation. It's easy to fake, but it's impossible to effectively have one without the other. Those who walk authentically in the demonstration of self-love also carry self-confidence, that type of dynamic is hard to recreate.

So to answer the initial question, it's not the self-confidence we lack, it's the sincere self-love that satisfies our searching.

Now that I've prepped you. Let me give you my 7 Keys to Self Confidence

When naming everything we love, sometimes it takes us a while before we ever name ourselves! So, let's start off with this simple exercise. Name 10 things you love about yourself. If you cannot think of 10 yet, hopefully by the time you finish this book you will be able to fill in every missing number.

10 Things I love about myself:

1.
2.
3.
4.
5.
6.
7.
8.
9.
10.

Chapter 3

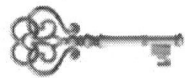

Key 1: Silence Negative Self Talk

"I can't do that!" "I'm the wrong one." "I'm not good at that." "I'm not smart enough." "I'm horrible at that." Do any of these phrases sound even remotely familiar to you? How often have you or do you currently speak these words to yourself?

I once saw a post online that said, "If a plant can grow by speaking kindly to it, imagine what you could do." Regardless to the exact science behind it, it's worth pontificating over and even practicing with yourself.

Often times, we are unaware of our inner voice that's speaking to us, feeding us negative opinions and information about ourselves.

It reminds us of how flawed we are. It tells us we're unattractive, unaccomplished, and insufficient, which then makes us insecure. The worst part about it is that we actually listen to it! We entertain ourselves by interacting in negative self-talk which in actuality is self-sabotaging behavior. We talk ourselves out of opportunities, healthy relationships. We blame haters not realizing that it's our own hesitancy holding us hostage from our very own words we are hearing.

You must first identify that the words you speak have the power to create and shape what you will soon see! Now, if you knew the words you were speaking had a direct correlation to the things you were seeing, and thus the life you were living, would you not adjust it accordingly? Let me ask again this way. If you knowingly realized that the life you want to live or even do not want to live is possessed in the power of what you release out of your mouth, then every word spoken whether verbally or mentally would first be weighed to determine if it's worth it.

Now understand that whether verbal or non-verbal, it still holds the same power. What you think will shape what you speak. The mind is the epicenter of the power. The scripture goes, "As a man thinketh in his heart, so is he." (Proverbs 23:7 KJV). That's not meant to be gender-specific, so he or she. Whomever! What you allow to slip into your heart will be what you think about, what you speak about, and what you will be about.

Wounds of Words

Sometimes the negative self-talk we speak is merely projections of what other people may have said to us or about us. It could have stemmed from as early as childhood where a parent or family member did not feed you with faithful words. Even relationships or friendships that failed you, but in return forced you to believe that you forfeited the rest of your life by not being with them. Maybe it was even an employer who caused you to think that you weren't even worth the cash they gave you. And because you had nothing else to counteract their negative words, you began to wrestle with the "what ifs" that exist within. As a result, sometimes you subconsciously became a product of the environmental influences that have been speaking to our psyche. We find ourselves believing that we can't do it, we'll never be good enough let alone enough. This is because we have allowed an enemy to infiltrate our focus and therefore penetrate our peace of mind.

We think that the old adage still stands that says, "Sticks and stones may break my bones, but words will never hurt me." There is nothing farther from the truth. Words have been the very thing that have created the wounds. Wounds that we yet wind up with for most of our lives. Maybe someone close to you carelessly told you things about yourself and on the inside, you said it wasn't you, but on the inside, you realized it was you. Now the real, real you, is still hiding beneath those isolated words as you replay them over and over as if you're trying to convince yourself otherwise.

This is what you will have to do. You have to forgive them for planting the words, then forgive yourself for believing them. Understand that it is true, "hurt people, hurt people." Sometimes the negative words spoken towards you were words someone once had spoken to them. Either way, it's time to silence them.

Magnify or Minimize

With talking about negative self-talk, we must briefly address additional cognitive distortions that are distracting us from effectively cultivating confidence. To simplify the term, I can best define it by saying, basically you are out here being lied to by your own brain. Get out of your own head!!! Our brain will cause us to make connections to very isolated things that should not hold merit together. Two that stick out most to me when working with women specifically during coaching sessions is magnifying and minimizing.

In hearing the word magnify, the first thing that can come to mind is what you do with a magnifying glass. You take it and make something that was once small and made to be small, and you enlarge it in a way that allows you to see it on a larger scale. This is what we do with problems we encounter, mistakes we make, and even the things others say or do. We will disrupt our own peace by focusing on these things that should seemingly be less significant and not hold much weight. Instead, we make them larger than life and tell ourselves all kinds of things as a result of it.

As an example, I may be in conversation with someone and second-guessed my every word later, and tell myself the person probably hates me now or thinks I'm crazy, maybe because of something I said or did. Even as a public speaker, I could have had an amazing presentation that was confirmed by those who expressed they were impacted by it, and instead of me giving myself credit for accomplishing the mission, I would be upset because I forgot to say one of my points on the paper. As a result, I've now slipped into a situational depression by telling myself how forgetful or unprofessional I am because I missed a point or thought. This all contributes to negative self-talk.

It's taking a simple flaw that you may consider the worst thing ever, and allowing it to control every aspect of your life, when in actuality it's really not that bad.

On the reverse, when we practice minimizing, we begin to downplay the amazing attributes and characteristics that makeup who we are. Using my own example, I will magnify my seemingly forgetful memory, and yet minimize my public speaking abilities to boldly stand before an entire crowd of people and present and empower an entire group of people. The decision I make to be dismissive of the positive parts of me and instead portray myself as a failure in my mind is toxic behavior in itself. If you are not careful, you will create an unhealthy habit which will prohibit you from that confidence you so desire.

To keep actualizing self-confidence, you have to first start with silencing that negative self-talk. Negativity only breeds and attracts more negativity, therefore, becoming the very toxicity in your life that you need to let go of. This will rob you of any confidence that you are trying to develop or produce.

The more I spoke to myself about myself, I began to acquire the confidence to believe what I was speaking. If you have nothing kind to say about yourself, don't say anything nor think anything. I once heard someone say, "It's not about what happens to you, it's the story that you tell yourself." What narrative have you been telling yourself lately?

It's time to unlearn these behaviors and counteract them with a strategy.

Self-Reflect

What is the most common negative self-talk I tell myself?

_____

When do I notice I engage in this behavior the most?

_____

What has caused me to not think highly of myself?

_____

What have I negatively magnified the most lately?

_____

What are the positive qualities about myself that I have minimized lately?

_____

CHAPTER 4

KEY 2: AFFIRM & CONFIRM

"I AM healthy, I am Whole, I am Healed."

It's important to create a positive counterattack against the negative self-talk. We've confronted those thoughts that should not be there, now it's time to replace them. I am a very action-oriented and get it done kind of girl. So, I cannot present you with a problem without following it up with allowing you the opportunity to find your solution, that just wouldn't be good for a goal strategist and life coach like myself to do. Personally, I'm repelled when others do it to me as well. I am committed to helping you on this journey and development.

Therefore, I want to present you with key number 2 and empower you to silence the negative self-talk with affirming and confirming. You do this by practicing positive self-talk also known as affirmations. Affirmations will be a game changer for shifting your mindset. It will begin to condition you for everything else that is to come and learn. I just need you to be open-minded to the concept and work behind using them.

FICTION or NAH?

Yes, there is a science to affirmations, but no, it is not magic, unfortunately. Therefore, it does not magically give you everlasting confidence and victory over all vices and negative voices for that matter, but there is a theory to it suggesting that it does expand our minds to become more flexible in our way of thinking and viewing ourselves. I won't get into the components of the self-affirmation theory, but it is widely respected and confirmed through neuroscientific research to substantiate the validity of it all. In other words, all I'm saying is the practice works, but only if you work it. So, this isn't just something that's trendy or just looks great to do, to post for the gram. It has to become an adopted way of life to actually talk positive, kind, and affirming to yourself. It's almost amazing, there has to be science to kindness, and yet here we are discussing it.

Nevertheless, one of the most beneficial projects my clients enjoy doing, is creating and customizing affirmations. Reciting and believing affirmations you speak assists with cognitive dissonance which takes place when you begin to feel in internal conflict between your thoughts and your actions when you know the two are not in alignment. Since it is natural for us as human beings to try and work towards consistency in our values in comparison to our actions, we can help reduce cognitive dissonance by practicing affirmations. Eventually something inside of you will have a desire to fix what is causing you a conflict in the words you are speaking to yourself and the actions that do not reflect those words.

Why is this so important?

Remember how we stated in Key 1, that the words you speak are a direct correlation to the thoughts you think. Your words are power, and once you have spoken something out of your mouth, you cannot retract it. It has now been sent on an assignment to accomplish the very thing you have said. So, what if you could replace those with something positive? You would then begin to use the power you possess to produce peace, prosperity, patience. This all boosts your self-confidence because you would then begin to believe it, speak it, and ultimately see it. And although it's true, "seeing is believing," you have to be able to see it taking place within yourself before you can ever see it happening for yourself. You have to have the discipline and the desire to claim it for yourself and then begin to align yourself with the actions to achieve it. We spend a significant amount of time thinking of what we are not instead of actualizing who we are or even have the potential to be, but we have to couple the desire with the discipline it will take. Let's put more affirmation into action.

So, before creating affirmations, it's a good practice to think of and write out everything negative you find yourself saying, thinking, or believing. Now, once you have written those things down, for every negative thought you have, create an opposite and positive "I AM" statement, to take its place. When you make those statements, you must practice them daily. I teach my clients to record themselves saying their affirmations out loud and play them back every day, and specifically in those moments, they may need an extra boost of confidence to confirm that they can and will get something done.

Allow them to resonate from the time you wake up, get dressed, drive in your car, and return home again. By the time your head hits the pillow, you should rest with assurance that you did the very best you could do that day, and that alone was, is, and will always be more than enough.

It is important that you learn to affirm and confirm yourself, then you will not seek it from others. When you don't seek it from others, you withdraw the power they once possessed as you press into the best version of yourself. There are also positive benefits to health. And we know when you feel better, you think better and vice versa. You actually think you can overcome anything and become anyone.

Let's Affirm

There is a category for every type of affirmation you need. That could be healing, happiness, home life, or just holistically. As a best practice, when creating your own affirmations, they should be positive, personal, and in the present tense. Time to erase the negative and reinforce the positive. For starters, most commonly affirmations can begin with two words: I am… Whatever you choose to put after them, will begin to shape your whole life. Let's try it, shall we? Then as you get a feel for them, begin to create more statements and positive affirming sentences to confirm the confidence on the inside of you.

Additional tips:

- Try recording yourself reciting your affirmations and play them every day for yourself.
- Utilize the mirror when affirming yourself. Look deeply beyond your surface and allow your spirit to resonate with every word you say until you believe and feel it.
- For every negative thought that arises, find a way to reverse it into the positive.

Try Putting These in An "I Am" Statement...

Abundant	Accepted
Mind-Blowing	Zealous
Innovative	Accomplished
Bold	Desirable
Brilliant	Productive
Beautiful	Fruitful
Calm	Diligent
Caring	Considerate
Dauntless	Established
Happy	Positive
Courageous	Healed
Optimistic	Intelligent
Blessed	Genius
Captivating	Purposed
Grateful	Effective

Brave	Ambitious
Determined	

My Own Personal Affirmations:

CHAPTER 5:

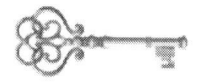

KEY 3: NAVIGATE SOMETHING NEW

"When was the last time you tried something new for the very first time?"

When I began to embark on my entrepreneurial journey, I had no idea that it would be in the areas of coaching, speaking, and writing books. I honestly did not know I even possessed those skills and abilities, but neither did I try. I just knew that I was after something in life and there was more that had to be in store. It was not until I tried something! I started with something I enjoyed which was fashion and accessories. I took that enjoyment and decided to be a jewelry consultant and grow my own personal business. Guess what happened? I failed miserably. I had no passion or desire for selling jewelry like I had for just wearing it. I had already made the investment in my package, purchased my domain name, and set up shop. I had friends who were so successful at it that I just knew it would work for me too! Unfortunately, it did not! But guess what it did do? It put a greater hunger in me and even a sense of confidence to know, "This may not be it, but something is!"

By changing my perspective and stepping outside myself, in a short amount of time, I've acquired and even developed multiple skill sets, talents, gifts, and even streams of income. All by making the decision to navigate something new, which gave me the confidence to dig deeper. I would often say the things that I was not good at or capable of, but I never actually took the action to see if that was even true or not.

Most of the time we become accustomed to doing everything the same way every day. Because we are creatures of habit, it's much easier to stick to what we do, than it is to try something new. Have you ever considered that when you do something that you never thought was possible for you to do, that you tap into a level of confidence you didn't know was possible for you? There is a sense of accomplishment or even the thought of the possibilities that could be. We stagnate ourselves by choosing to live stiff! Staying still. Doing the same thing, the same way, every single day. We are quick to say what we cannot do, but we never take the time to discover what we can do. One way to boost confidence is to try something new. Now, this may not seem very significant to you, but it is. Trying and learning new things is a great way to boost your confidence. You don't have to be great at it but stepping outside your comfort zone shows your versatility and your capability of doing something different. You may surprise yourself with what skills you may discover in the process, or even enjoy. Navigating or trying something new not only expands your capacity to grow, it also develops a greater sense of self. You will tap into another level of confidence you didn't have.

Try this on!

Sometimes navigating something new starts with making small and little changes and adjustments in your life. It could be so simple as trying a new way while driving, trying a new lip color, or maybe even doing your hair in a different style. When was the last time you updated your wardrobe and tried a different style? Entertaining the idea of something new doesn't mean you have to marry the idea, It simply means that you have enough confidence to go for it! You don't always have to make huge drastic changes. It is the simple things that play such a huge difference in your confidence level. Who knows if that little change or act of faith is the very catalyst and stepping stone to the confidence you're trying to activate.

7 Keys to Self-Confidence

If you want a level of confidence you've never had before, you are going to have to do some things you have never done before. If you knew that you could not fail, what is it that you would do? What are you waiting for?

What are 3 new things I can try now?

1._____

2._____

3._____

CHAPTER 6:

4 FIND A POSITIVE POSSE

"If you want to go quickly, go alone. If you want to go far, go together." ~African Proverb

I have my own saying that "The company that you keep will reflect in the person that you will turn out to be." Often times we don't' realize that who we choose to be around will weigh us down. If you are not a person who complains often or seems to always have a chip on their shoulder towards someone, surround yourself with someone who does, and sooner or later, you will find yourself becoming just like them and not even realize it.

I once had to double take on those in Destiny's life! The more I became self-aware, I realized that some of my behavior patterns were reflective of the people I allowed to be in place. Many relationships I had to make the decision to allow them to dissolve before my destiny was dismantled as a result of them. It was very painful and even lonely in certain seasons, but I knew what I was after and what I needed to help me obtain it. When I became a more positive person who remained pure, I was able to attract the positive people I truly needed in my posse. I was then perfectly positioned. Their love and positivity were priceless.

You have to take an inventory of your environment and identify those who are not contributing to the process of growth and change that you desperately desiring in your life. It does not mean they are bad people, it could be that their influence in your life is just bad in comparison to where it is you are trying to go, and who it is that you wish to be.

Don't be alarmed if you begin to outgrow the people in your posse. It does not mean that you are pushing them out, it means that when you are purposed, you have to only pursue and be pursued by those who fit that purpose. The right posse will push you into heights unknown. They will be able to pull out things inside of you that you did not even know existed. The opposite can be said of those who are negative influences in your life.

When I say negative influence it does not mean that they themselves are even negative people. It just means that the part they play in your life does not positively serve you. Do they live life limitless or are they lazy? Do they affirm your destiny or help you make bad decisions?

Do they lift up others or do they lie on them? These are all things you have to consider about a posse because they possess the power to help your confidence or lead you further into a state of chaos. Consider that you can't go farther in life, because there are some people attached to you that are so accustomed to foolishness.

Having positive influences in my circle really helped me push me to the next level. My father once told me, "Either they are going to draw you, or you are going to draw them." Once he told me that I became obsessed with being drawn by those who represented where I wanted to go and not just where I had been. Those who inspired, empowered, and ignited the flame within me.

Your posse, team, tribe, circle, or whatever you refer to them as, should consist of those who are invested in your growth. They should want to see you win at life. This should be your go-to support system. They may not have the same career, goals, or social status. Nevertheless, there should be alignment in your values and where you are headed in life. If not, a part of your confidence as well as your destiny may be sacrificed or even jeopardized by trying to hold on to something that is not headed where you are going, which is up.

Here's a few more pointers about a positive posse. They won't allow negativity to occupy the same space. They won't allow you to settle for mediocrity. They will constantly build you up and boost your confidence and also call you out on the carpet when needed. You have to be in a place to be receptive of them, but that's why you equally have to know who deserves that place in your posse.

The energy and synergy of a positive posse is incomparable. Not only do they pour into you, but you positively pour back into them. They are the people you are allowing to feed your spirit. Even the natural food you eat contributes to the energy you will have. What you consume from your posse will never leave you drained.

DO YOU HAVE A POSITIVE POSSE?

Evaluate your circle of influence by tracking the answers to these questions:

1. Are your friends or acquaintances high achievers?
2. Do those around you root for you when you win and encourage you when you lose?
3. Are they consistent with positively pouring into you?
4. Is your life made better just by their presence?
5. Do your friends only run to you with the "tea?" Or do they themselves "have the juice?" In other words, are they bringing you information that can level you up?
6. Do your friends co-sign on drama, praise your poor decisions, and watch your self-destructive behaviors?
7. Do your friends push you out of your comfort zone or encourage you to stay complacent?

    Are your friends as equally supportive of you if not more, as you are towards them? If so, how do they prove it?

8. Do you ever feel the need to pretend or go along with the things that are said or done, but on the inside, you really are not in agreement with it?

9. Do you ever have a gut feeling about people in your posse, but you can't quite put your finger on what it is about them?

Really consider the answers to these questions. When you know the outcome, decide if you are ready to make the adjustments.

Ask Yourself:

What will happen if I don't make the adjustments to my posse and those I allow in my personal environment?

_____

_____

_____

How is my current circle of influence impacting my life?

_____

_____

_____

CHAPTER 7:

KEY 5: HONOR YOUR HEALTH

To honor is to respect. When you respect something, you handle it with care and concern. Have you ever noticed how typically we tend to focus our attention on everything but our health? Every year, billions of dollars are made in the beauty industry worldwide. We love to feel, look, and be beautiful on the outside and we will spare no expense or time to do so until we feel good about ourselves. There is absolutely nothing wrong with this. Hair, nails, brows, lashes on fleek every day of the week! But when you put more emphasis on what's only on the outside and not equally what's on the inside, then you are unbalanced. It is difficult to walk in the most confident and authentic version of yourself when you are not holistically in a place of health.

To speak quite candidly, I tried to find my confidence

in caking on makeup and having a beat face in order to feel beautiful. I was suffering silently on the inside. Hurting on the inside but trying to help others on the outside. Feeding my face in depression or even starving myself in oppression. As a result, I looked confident, but my mind was full of concerns, I was not truly honoring my health holistically.

Health is not just determined by how you look on the outside. It's the intentionality of what you do and put on the inside of you. This Earth suit is not just flesh, it is a temple. The most sacred temple you will ever encounter. It should be treated as such! From what you put in it to what you do with it.

What we don't realize is that health plays the biggest part. Much of how we see ourselves comes from how we feel about ourselves. How we feel about ourselves will show in how we choose to honor and take care of ourselves.

Types of Health

Just so we're clear, when I say health I am not just referring to eating celery and checking the numbers on a scale. No! This may include that, but it is so much bigger. When I say honor your health, I'm referencing mental health, emotional health, spiritual health, in addition to physical health. I know what it feels like to have a flawless "face beat" to the makeup "gawds," yet toss and turn at night. Mentally, I was carrying the burdens of all my mistakes. I wasn't intentional in my movements because my emotions were a complete mess. Spiritually, I felt like a piece of me was dying daily. I was drained! I was not in divine alignment with what I call in my first book *Discovering Destiny* as my divine assignment. There was consistently pieces of me that were missing, which caused me to seek to fill these voids that I thought were beyond my control. There was a disconnect and it was not well within my soul. I was not honoring my temple, my mind, nor caring for my emotional health. When I understood the connection between these areas of my life, I was then able to create synergy which gave me a healthy energy! This energy not only flowed but showed throughout my life for others to see.

You have to remember that we are mind, body, and soul. You cannot compartmentalize which parts of your health you deem most important to focus on. You have to devote time with each area of yourself that makes up the total you. So, make sure you are intentional with honoring it. Each has a domino effect with the ability to take you to another level in your development and growth.

Begin unlocking confidence by creating healthy habits and routines. Put systems and disciplines in place and make a commitment to stick to them. It's hard to look good if you don't feel good! How refreshing does it feel when you know you are healed? Because healing is a process, do not worry if it doesn't happen overnight. Sis, that is alright. What is important is that you are walking towards wholeness in so many areas of your life. You can confidently say, "I am healthy, I am whole, and I am healed."

When you feel good about yourself, you exhibit more confidence that not only you will notice, but also will also radiate around you. A whole you, is a healthy You! A healthy you is a you who is able to now help others heal. Honor your health.

WAYS TO HONOR YOUR HEALTH

MENTAL	PHYSICAL
Pray & Meditate Daily	Get Regular Check-Ups
Decompress At The End Of Each Day	Go For A Walk Once A Week
Get Therapy/Counseling	Exercise Regularly
Journal Your Thoughts	Drink Plenty Water
Read books	Give Your Body Plenty Rest
Listen to audio books	Eat A Balanced Diet
Find informative articles & blogs	Take Vitamins
Listen to Podcasts Play Positive Music	Do Consistent Self-Checks

CHAPTER 8

KEY 6: IGNORE NEGATIVITY

I choose what gets to take up real estate in my reality! Negativity is a hard NO!"

Currently, in the year 2020, it would appear that simply everything that could go wrong has went wrong or has the potential to still go wrong. Every news, media, and social outlet has presented content that penetrates and pierces every part of our hearts. If you are not careful, you will begin to buy into what they are selling. It is important to unplug from all of the problems around you. It's hard to be confident about your future and anticipate a reversal of a poor fortune if you never ignore the negativity. It does not mean that you pretend it's not real, but it means you will not let negativity negate the destiny for your life. That alone is enough to have confidence in.

Very simple, we have already unlocked the key of having a positive posse, so it goes without saying that sometimes people will try to spew negative poisonous venom and crush the confidence we are trying so desperately to curate. This is not always done intentionally, however, some people are negative by nature and you, so you have to know when to say NO to that. Otherwise, they will draw you into a place that you cannot protect your peace from.

Notes about negativity

1. Negativity drains you
2. Weakens your immune system
3. Blinds you from what's before you
4. Robs you of positive possibilities
5. Causes you to repel people that are not replaceable
6. Can potentially lead to depression
7. Creates low level living
8. Makes you miss out on special moments
9. Distracts you from your destiny
10. Robs you of what is rightfully yours

Any space, place, or person that spews negativity is counterproductive to your confidence. Ignore it! Don't even follow it up. Negativity can come from our work environment, school, home, social media, or on the news. The effects can be dangerous.

Don't allow thoughts, opinions, words, and the actions of others to cause you to look at your life differently. There is no reason to feel less than or discouraged by the negativity of your environment. You are phenomenal whether someone else has the capacity to see it and regardless of what's going on in the world around us. Fix your focus only on what feeds and fuels your confidence!

Reflect:

What are things that you notice put you in a negative frame of mind?

1. _____

2. _____

3. _____

What is an action you can take when you notice negativity present in your life?

_____
_____

CHAPTER 9:

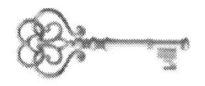

KEY 7: EXPECT THE BEST

"The outer conditions of a person's life will always be found to be harmoniously related to his inner state. Men do not attract that which they want, but that which they are." James Allen

Have you ever noticed a season of your life where things would go wrong and instantly your initial thought was "I knew it was too good to be true?" I want to take you back to our earlier keys when we discussed the power of thoughts and the power of words. You program yourself to begin to draw disappointment because you have no expectation set. Often times our reticular activator kicks in which causes us to notice things that will confirm our negative belief of an outcome. These are the nerves in our brainstem that allows us to focus on what is most important to us. As a result, we can block or filter anything else out.

everything else. An example of this is deciding you want a red sports car. Now every time you are driving you are spotting red sports cars. Did the abundance of red cars change? Or did you notice them more because your Reticular Activating System kicked in? A helpful way that you can align these subconscious thoughts is by setting an intention or expectation.

There is a level of confidence acquired when you have an expectation for things that are unexplainable. You have to use the key of expectation to tap into confidence to believe who you are and what you can have. Expect that you are the type of person who deserves what they are expecting.

Contrary to popular belief, I don't plan for the best and expect the worse. I constantly position myself to expect great things to happen to me and for me. I expect the best and therefore, I'm prepared for it when it comes! I expect the very thing I am anticipating. I once had a friend who would consistently tell me "No expectation no disappointment." True, when we do not see the thing we so desire, it can bring about a disappointment. However, when you understand season and time, you don't try to tame your expectation. If it happens, then it goes as planned, nevertheless, if it doesn't happen, I can tap into an even greater level of confidence that affirms me that I am one step closer to it.

Average people accept life as it is given to them and therefore, their level of confidence is indicative of such low-level thinking. Average people walk around expecting the worst as a way to avoid disappointment.

As a person who chooses to walk in authority, power, and confidence, I decide on what I desire, and I put that expectation into the atmosphere. I choose to live my life above average! I think and expect the absolute best. I believe in the impossible, because the very spelling of the word declares that "I'm possible." Therefore, I have an anticipation of a divine manifestation. That takes an entirely new level of self-confidence to believe that you possess that kind of power. I like to call it Killer Confidence. This kind of confidence kills out doubt, insecurity, unbelief, fear, and any other barrier blocking the destination. Average minds can't maintain!

Does this mean everything turns out perfectly? Of course not! But I set the expectation for my life high yet reasonable! When you put positivity out, that's what you expect in return. Manifestation! I visualize what I want, I tell myself I am worthy of it, and I work to ensure it happens.

Your level of expectation determines your elevation.

Is your expectation in alignment with the life you want start living?

Expect to be treated with respect.

Expect a promotion.

Expect good things to happen around you.

Expect your fortune to turn in your favor.

Expect what seems impossible for others to be possible for you. You've already experienced the worse, now expect the best.

It's more than just an expectation. It works in collaboration with the dedication that you will put forth to see it. This is the key to tapping into self-confidence. Try creating mental pictures in your mind of what you want an outcome to be. Even practicing visualization can be helpful. Let your subconscious mind begin to go to work to filter out everything that is not a part of your expectation. If you can tune out the color of every other car on the road besides the red car, then surely you are capable of focusing your mind to tune out negative outcomes and expectations. Again, you are aligning your actions with the thoughts to produce the desired outcomes.

I Expect The Best:

List what you are bold enough to expect the best concerning. Decide what your plan of action will be.

Expectation	Action Plan

By now you are fully equipped with 7 dynamic keys that if followed through consistently and intentionally will help you tap into a higher level of self-confidence! Keys are meant to unlock doors. The keys presented to you should not only help you unlock confidence but also opportunity. Opportunity that will allow you to do better, think better, and be better. Also unlock the gifts and purpose on the inside of you that has been lying dormant all along. Just know that you are deserving of every good thing that comes your way. You are capable of becoming the person you are purposed to be. You will be able to go after that job, shoot your shot, change the climate of the world around you, and be exactly who you were called to be. Ultimately, I want you to feel good about the masterpiece that you are.

With authentic self-confidence, you are capable of accomplishing feats unknown! Your light will become contagious and radiate in the world around you. Elevating the life of everyone you come in contact with.

I already believe in you, now it's time you believed in yourself! Trust yourself, your abilities, and your judgment. Confidently walk towards the directions of your goals and never look back. It's time you stopped limiting your expectations and begin to think, dream, and live limitless.

The Conclusion of the Matter

Confidence is and will always be an inside job. It is not contingent upon anyone else besides the individual who seeks it. One of the greatest keys of self-confidence you will ever hear is knowing that you are a creation of the greatest architect in the world. You were formed and created in the image of a divine and supreme being who loved you so much, He sent his son to die for your sins. That knowledge coupled with the content in this book should help kickstart you with the confidence you need to conquer any and everything that comes your way. I am so excited for your journey as the King or Queen you were always called to be!

If this book has helped to inspire or empower you in any way, I challenge you to pay it forward and sow it as a good seed into the life of someone else who too may be on their journey to cultivating their confidence.

Aren't you ready to live the life you not only desire to live but were designed to live? You deserve it! You alone have the answers on the inside of you. Sometimes you only have to dig deep enough to ask yourself powerful questions to bring the answers out of you. The next level of your life is contingent upon your ability to believe in yourself and develop the self-confidence you need. If you are one who finds yourself overthinking at times, allow yourself to sink into your heart space. Now allow yourself to connect them together and find the balance between what you know to be true! Time to stop limiting your life and start unlocking your next level. You now have the self-confidence to do it!

Do you remember the list of 10 things you love about yourself? I want you to ask yourself, what do you now love about yourself? Compare your two lists and see what all changed. Additionally, answer the powerful coaching questions at the end of this book. I am confident that within you is lying the answers that you are seeking for. Remember you have the all-powerful one on the inside. I want to empower you to look within instead of always looking without. It is my hope that you have a little more confidence after much reflection and answering powerful questions. If nobody has told you yet, allow me to be the first. I am so proud of you!

10 Things I now love about myself:

1.
2.
3.
4.
5.
6.
7.
8.
9.
10.

Ask yourself these powerful coaching questions:

What will happen if I don't become a more confident version of myself?

What would happen if I did gain more self-confidence?

What is it I could accomplish?

What is stopping me from self-confidence?

What do I now need to give myself permission to do?

What was my aha moment while reading this book?

What key do I need to work on the most?

Notes: Reflection Space

Notes: Reflection Space

Destiny Kingcannon, known as Destiny Inspire, is a master certified life coach, consultant, author, award-winning speaker, and founder of The Queen Counsel Women Empowerment Community. She is passionate about serving women through to help them improve their quality of life, convert their pain into power, and walk in their God-given purpose. She also provides coaching, consulting and empowerment services to corporations, schools, universities, non-profit organizations, and church organizations. She would love to provide value for you. She is sure to help facilitate your desired process of growth and change. Connect with her at www.destinyinspire.com.

Download the app *Crowned by Destiny Inspire.*

The ultimate women empowerment app and a safe space for women globally. Available in App Store and Google Play. Time to get officially crowned.